MW01102095

Beautifully Empowered

The Gift of Gratitude

Natasha Mochrie

Beautifully Empowered

The Gift of Gratitude

Natasha Mochrie

Beautifully Empowered

 Daring to Share Global

Published by Beautifully Empowered Publishing
April 2022 ISBN: 9781778120305

Editor: John De Freitas
Typeset: Greg Salisbury
Book Cover Design: Olli Vidal

Dedication

Think of a time you told someone how grateful you were for their help, support, or even just for being in your life. Maybe you can remember when someone gave you something you didn't buy or ask for as a token of gratitude. It felt pretty good, didn't it?

This book is for every individual out there who wants to express their love in themselves and towards others. How you practice the act of gratitude while learning to appreciate the Beautifully Empowered emotions that accompany it.

May you always see strength from every mirror you walk by while looking back at yourself. May you feel that childhood-like spirit you once held tightly. Be the heart with no worries. Be the peace and carefree spirit you may have lost growing up. Be your own hero and cherish the time you have because tomorrow isn't promised, and yesterday became a what if.

Praise

Beautifully Empowered is a true caterpillar to butterfly narrative. Natasha speaks with raw honesty and courage, sharing her journey as to how she came to terms with an event that would profoundly alter her life. While Natasha found herself falling into a downward spiral of depression, she learned to embrace her emotions and received them as "gifts." By doing so, Natasha gives insight as to how she came to accept and overcome each obstacle that threatened to prevent her from moving forward in her healing journey. I feel privileged to know Natasha and to have witnessed the "butterfly" that emerged as a result of her courage. I look forward to following her journey of growth in the years to come.

~Ryan Carlisle
Lead Counsellor & Owner,
Game Changers Counselling Co.

Natasha's book is heartfelt, deep, and inspiring. It grabs you from the start, she tells her story like she would to a friend and grabs your attention from the start and doesn't let go. A true testimony for young people everywhere to awaken to a better life.

~Abe Salmon
Investor, Entrepreneur, Mentor.

Once I started reading Natasha's story, I couldn't put it down. I was invested in every word, every sentence, and every chapter. The story brought me to tears and also gave me joy and hope, knowing that her story will inspire and help others who are going through pain, suffering, loss, depression and there truly is light at the end of the tunnel. Her story of her mom singing "You're my sunshine", took me back to the times when I sang the same to my girls. We all want what is best for our children and Natasha's story brings so much hope and courage to families who may be going through tough times.

Gordon So
Co-Founder, Landed for Success

Gratitude

Thank you to all who travelled through my madness,
helping me see the light through my pain and sorrow.

To my lighthouse,
thank you for leading me home in more ways
than I could hope.

To my mentors,
thank you for giving me knowledge and perspective.

To my family,
thank you for never losing hope even during
the most dire times.

To my beautiful angel,
who I never held, never got to kiss
or had the chance to name,
I know one day I will see you again
and meet the beautiful mirror image of myself.
You were a gift never brought to life,
but I thank you for the gift of life you gave me.

Most of all,
special thanks to my beautiful monarch butterfly, Brenda,
and my brother, Adam, who always shows me kindness
and makes sure my dreams become a reality.

Foreword

First and foremost, I would like to express my gratitude to Natasha for asking me to write the foreword for this remarkable journey you are about to experience. You see, I didn't know this beautiful soul before her words were eloquently written. I didn't have the opportunity to truly understand the part of her that changed. I only see what I see now, which is why I truly believe that the title of this book is so significant. I see the beautifully empowered woman who fought one of the hardest battles a person can possibly fight—the battle within oneself.

When I hear the statement, *Stroke Survivor*, I think of a person remaining alive after an event in which others have died. However, although they remain alive, are they still truly living? Natasha states this while going through her *recovery* grieving process, and it made me think about the comments I most frequently received during my early recovery, *wow, you look great. It looks like you made a full recovery in a short time.* I wondered, *does anyone ever make a full recovery?*

I agree with her perspective. No one is the same person they were yesterday, but I am not here to lessen the ordeal that she went through with that statement. She went through more than most can ever imagine at such a young age. However, through forced introspection and detachment, she realized that part of the person she was originally no longer existed. This new reality was not based on a state of victimhood but rather from a victor's awareness that this event didn't happen to her but for her. The only choice she had was to work on herself, which is a choice that many take for granted, and in many cases, avoid doing. When forced to stop and look at her life, she knew the direction she had to move in, courageously moving toward the resistance instead of running away from it.

Being vulnerable enough to tap into the discipline needed to discover your authentic self can only be achieved by the willing. It cannot be forced upon someone. A person must want to find this alignment to discover the greatness within it. Although I only see a view from this side of the mirror, I know that the version she currently presents is aligned with her authenticity, which again takes courage—massive courage. It also takes a strong faith in the ability to overcome, regardless of what the outside world's reality attempts to impose. Therefore, I believe she is one of the strongest people I have ever met.

I am proud of her for the will and persistence she exemplified in this story you are about to experience. However, I am far prouder of the person who is not just a survivor. I am proud that she has accepted that she will never recover the version of her former self. I may not have known the Natasha of the past, but what I know that she is different. I refuse to normalize her based on her former self because, as hard as it is to comprehend what she went through, she has embraced her strengths and weaknesses in her current state, which is more than so many do.

The reflections and notes she wrote in this book paint an emotional picture in her most vulnerable state. They will take you through personal epiphanies about her and her loved ones in a way that brought me to tears. She will take you right there inside her cocoon of fear, comparison, and self-doubt with an overarching feeling of *What If*, along with the brutal reality of an uncertain future. Although she received the help she needed from her family and community, she also knew that this was a journey of independence. When she fell, she knew she had to pick herself up. No matter how hard the struggle was, she had to fly on her own.

From the first day I met Natasha, I quickly realized she was a beautifully empowered butterfly who refused to allow the circumstances of one earth-shattering moment hold her back from her journey. Instead of asking *why this happened to me*, she searched for the gift within the loneliness, pain, and struggle. These gifts are presented to you and me, the reader who will never truly understand what she went through. Thankfully, she was able to present her gratitude to us through her guidelines as an author, poet, and self-love coach. Based on her story alone, I cannot think of anyone more qualified to support others to become the best version of themselves by not relying on anyone else to pick them up.

Through sheer will and determination and by leading by example, she demonstrates that when life knocks you down, there really are only so many choices. Do you stay down or get back up? Do you choose to live or choose to die? Do you say yes to a positive direction, or do you say no? Natasha suffered a stroke; for many, their choice may have been to stay down, but not her. She is different because she made the choice to stand up and blatantly refused to accept the words of others who tried to impose their reality upon her. She chose to get back up and fly like the beautifully empowered butterfly that she is. And for that, we can choose to be grateful for her gift of gratitude.

Corey Laine Hilton, Author
Take It Off—Revelations of a Male Exotic Dancer
Authenticity Coach & Introspective Influencer
www.coreylainehilton.com
February 2022

Introduction

This motivational memoir will support you to be mindful and open to the process of personal evolution. The stories, thoughts, tips, and ideas I have shared in this narrative will support you to become a better version of yourself. I experienced a year that encompassed everything from sorrow to bliss, agony to joy, along with trauma to healing. It was extraordinarily uncomfortable, and yet, throughout it all, there was a shining light that continued to guide me to a place of peace when my mind became clouded and weary. I waited a long time to record my innermost reflections and lessons until one day when I decided to write them down to inspire my mindfulness journey.

The narrative you are about to absorb is a true story about how I found myself after losing all hope of living. These pages describe how I overcame the intense experience of almost dying while moving forward with a completely different view about living. It's about my dog, my closest companion, Rigg, and how his purity showed me something that cannot be seen through the naked eye but instead felt through the energy of love and courage.

My approach guides you to discover what old traumas affect how you present yourself to the people around you and how you can shift your way of being by resolving them. Each chapter features a self-reflection section at the end where you can delve deep into self-discovery and the gift of gratitude.

My question is: *Why wait until you're almost dead to live?* This is why this book is not just based on a series of chronological events or a journal filled with musings. Yes, it includes sadness and loss, poetry and sex, and the countless days I spent crying in pain and feeling distressed. But it also details the journey of transformation that took me from the old me to the upgraded, more confident, and authentic version. Each chapter provides a guideline that is part of a ten-step system I created that continues to guide me and that can support you. In detail, I share how the process worked for me and how significantly it can shift your mindset if you stick to it. The decision is entirely yours: to either improve your life or allow it to defeat you.

Pause for a second and think about the moment you lay down in bed to the moment you wake up; these are choices you make. In a perfect world, you then shower, get dressed, and brush your teeth. These are things you learned and became part of the beginning of your daily routine. But what if you couldn't physically or mentally do them anymore? What if everything that represented who you thought you were was taken away?

My name is Natasha Eve Lynne Mochrie. I was 31 when I had a stroke. I woke up one morning thinking I would carry on in my perfect little world. And then, everything I was taught to value and my choices led me to a hospital bed. I had a left vertebral artery dissection in the back of my neck—a cerebral stroke on the brain stem, causing deficits on both sides of my body. There was a painful blood clot involved, and for several minutes, my brain received no oxygen. To this day, it is unknown why this happened because, from a medical standpoint, the cause is genetic, women's birth control, or a massive head injury. None were the case for me. As astonishing as this was to my family and me, the doctors were also shocked.

It was a one-in-a-million incident that should have left me paralyzed or brain dead, but instead, I chose life. I chose me, and the universe gave me a second chance at life—I was not going to waste it. I truly believe everything happens for a reason, but we have the choice to live that purpose. Everything leading up to this life-altering event impacted how it played out—all the trauma, love, loss, and gains I experienced from when I was a toddler to a teenager, and especially through my adolescence, played a significant role in its trajectory.

Many spend a lifetime burying trauma because we are unaware of its scarring impact on us. As a human species, we are programmed to cope and suck it up. Although there is nothing wrong with moving through challenging life experiences that make us strong and wise, what is important is how we show up afterwards, with attributes like kindness, gratitude, and joy—three daily gratitude speeches that I resonate with.

It wasn't until a few months ago that I went back to read my journals. They were filled with scarcity and sadness, and things didn't start to change for the better until I expanded my mind and opened doors by surrounding myself with people who brought my natural light out. When we decide to make a difference in this one life we have, things begin to seem more extraordinary than ever. It starts with small goals and a willingness to shift one's mindset.

I am so grateful for every start to my day. I wake up to Big Rigg. He is my best friend with four paws and the one who saved my life. In the morning, he greets me with snuggles, and the minute I hear his little paws, my heart melts like an ice cube. Life feels good with Rigg in it. I know that not everyone has a pet or someone special to wake up to, but that is all the more reason to find something to be grateful for that brings joy in your heart.

You are alive. And in fact, yesterday's bottom line is gone, and a new day has begun. It is a gift to wake up to another day, one that you can discover and implement your life's purpose. If you can go to bed at night knowing you did the best to be kind towards the universe, that is all that matters.

As horrible as my stroke was, I was fortunate to have such a massive awakening. I felt reborn with a soulful journey and life's purpose. Everything I used to think was important flew by me and was mute: love, sex, friends, and all sorts of worldly things, even my old hobbies. None of it had the same meaning, and the people I had in my life didn't notice I was different. It was like I was me, but I wasn't. And yet, none of it bothered me because nothing was more meaningful than the fact that I was alive.

My wish for you is that you use the added space at the end of each chapter to reflect and write a letter to yourself or express who you are in a poem. You can take some time to share a heartfelt memory of either sorrow or happiness—a specific smell that took you back to a time you had forgotten or when tears ran down your cheeks because your heart fell into your stomach from emotional pain. Each chapter will stir up thoughts to produce a significant gift as you learn to detach from emotion, allowing the expansion and growth of your healing process. By letting go and using the inspiration of my story and the motivation of each guiding step, you will turn something negative into something beautifully empowering, and you will surrender to the abundance of gratitude.

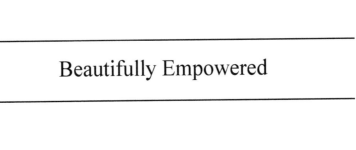

Beautifully Empowered

I

The Gift of Grief

To be inspired
is to be broken into one thousand pieces
and to feel that you can never be put back together again.
Inspired is to fall, but then rise.

~Natasha Mochrie

I was up early one Sunday morning on February 2, 2020. The sun was out, and I just finished a killer workout and walked my dog, Riggs, in my Kelowna, BC, neighbourhood. While relaxing and enjoying my tea on the couch, I thought about how I spent the night before with a friend, who was also my neighbour and boss's wife. We had dinner and a couple of drinks—nothing too crazy—and then went home early. I was happy for the early night and the chance to start my day off right. Big Rigg sat beside me on the couch when I suddenly began to feel nauseous and lightheaded. I thought, *Wow, what the hell is going on?*

Everything happened so fast that, to this day, I find pieces I blocked out. At about 10:30 in the morning, I remember looking at my phone because I was supposed to meet my girlfriend for lunch. I decided to lie down because I felt terrible, but Riggs started jumping and barking at me; I ignored him because I felt so sick. Riggs jumped onto the bed as I lay curled up, and I started getting irritated. He kept barking at me and nibbling at

1

my fingers. And then, to my surprise, he bit me, so I sat up and yelled at him, and it scared me into motion. He looked at me with such concern, and I started to shake and feel numb on the left side. Suddenly, I thought to myself, *Oh, SHIT, I am having a heart attack or stroke! No, there is no way I am having a stroke. I am only 31 years old! I am healthy and young!*

Riggs started barking again, and he was standing near my keys this time. I began to pace around my home, thinking, *Okay, if I can't stop shaking or that numbness doesn't stop, I'll go to the hospital.* Then I realized I couldn't feel my right side at all. I was petrified as I tried calling my neighbour and discovered that the phone lines were down. So, I decided to drive. For some people, the first thought in an emergency is to call 911. However, mine was to get to the hospital. I looked at Riggs, and he looked back at me with fear in his eyes. I grabbed my purse, looked at him and said, *Mom loves you. I'll be right back.* I didn't know it at the time, but I wouldn't see Riggs until almost a month later.

Adrenaline coursed through my body as I raced to the hospital. I was focused on my destination yet, at one point, I remember thinking, *Please God, save me and my eyebrows.* It seems laughable now, but the nurses said it was all I asked for, and my friends confirmed it later. The whole time I was driving, the one thing that concerned me was my eyebrows and my face being droopy on one side. I am not sure how I didn't crash my car in my death-defying race to the hospital.

A block away from my destination, I managed to call 911 and tell someone my name and that I was pretty sure I was having a heart attack or stroke. He told me to pull over and wait, not knowing what most people know about me: I am a strong-minded and very stubborn woman. I said, *Well, I am almost there*, and hung up and kept driving. Surprisingly, I managed to park my car and walk in unassisted. I thought I was steady but was later told that I came in limping and said, I'm having a stroke, and then passed out.

After an unknown period of time, a doctor put me in a wheelchair, and a clerk took my identification and noticed I could talk a bit. I was then put in a trauma room. Shit got real after that. It was a blur back then, but clear as day 11 months later. I sat on the hospital bed in an emergency room with wires hooked up to me, listening to three nurses who kept saying I was fine. I kept pinching my skin, saying I couldn't feel my right side and that my left side was heavy. But they still wouldn't listen to me. Finally, in desperation, I pulled off my top, ripped out my nipple piercing, indicating that I couldn't feel anything, and said, *This isn't right! Please help me. There is something wrong!*

Because I knew something was wrong with me, and I needed immediate attention and wasn't receiving it, I didn't trust that the doctors and nurses were providing thorough care. I went to sleep for a while, and when I woke up, I realized I had been in the trauma room for five days. I wasn't sure where I was, and I couldn't see or move my body. I was weak and not fully conscious but heard the emergency doctor who initially treated me apologizing to me for his mistake—for missing the window to give me a blood thinner that could have prevented my stroke. This caused the blood clot in my neck. Despite blood work and two CT scans, he and others missed what was really going on. When I first questioned them, medical staff continuously told me there was nothing they could do for me, that I was okay, and that I should go home and lie down. I told the doctor I did not have vertigo like he suggested, and I refused to leave until I was treated. Then, they wheeled me out into the hallway under the lights. I remember the endless minutes, the people, and the bright agonizing lights, but most of all, I remember the most excruciating pain of my life.

Lying there, blind and paralyzed, I heard someone asking, *How long have her eyes been like this? How long has she been vomiting? How long has she been having a seizure?* It was an out-of-body experience whereby I was aware of everything happening, but I couldn't respond; I wondered over and over what I had done to deserve this. Finally, I was able to tell the doctor that I knew something was wrong and remembered people walking past me. All he said to me was that he was sorry I went through that. He was sorry! I couldn't understand how someone could be sorry yet do nothing. I lay in a bed, unable to move, unable to see, and listened to my heartbeat like it was being pulled out of my chest. I couldn't trust them. They didn't listen to me tell them there was something wrong. There were nurses, paramedics, the entire staff attending to me, and even a neurologist later on. Still, I wasn't satisfied with their diagnosis and the degree of medical care they gave me. I felt I knew my body better than those trying to diagnose me.

After my stroke, I constantly thought about what I might miss out on. My doctor gave me a huge list of activities I couldn't do. I started thinking about the people who probably wouldn't want to hang out with me anymore. I had a lot of time to think about people in my life and things I was attached to. I learned who my true friends are. Among them is my dog. Big Rigg is the most meaningful and loving attachment I have. He helped me get through the most challenging times when I felt overtaken by grief.

Grief was a cold dark feeling of loss and abandonment. It showed up as fear of what I could be missing out on, yet in reality, it was just an emotion—a blockage in my mind. I was attached to a number of things, and when they were gone, I felt loss and pain. I was attached to people, the person I used to be, and the life I always expected to be safe and predictable. I learned that after trauma, grief can cause physical, cognitive, and behavioural problems. I was never taught how to manage fear, and I didn't automatically know how to deal with emotional issues and trauma. Help appeared in various forms: talking to someone professionally, accessing online resources, or taking medications. For me, turning to medication cut me off emotionally and didn't always lead to closure. Being outside and learning to ground myself in nature helped—I immersed myself in it, energizing my mind, and cleansing my spirit .

Reflection

After the stroke, my brain scrambled to be put back together, so I went on anti-depressants and anti-anxiety pills that made me feel even more confused and depressed for six months. They numbed me, and I felt like I lost more of myself each day. During moments of despair, I remember holding onto things and people so tightly that I became stuck in limbo and forgot how happy I was before my attachment. I felt selfish for believing I was entitled to keep that person or experience, even though I knew it was the right thing to let go. I find it's never easy to say goodbye, but I learned that when one door closes, others open. I realized it was okay to hold on, and it was okay to love to a depth only I could understand. But my fear of loss made anything that came into my life feel short-term. I watched people, jobs, and materialistic things come and go, and I treasured them because I knew nothing was permanent. The change was scary but necessary for my growth.

The most frequent comment I received during my early recovery was, *Wow, you look great. It looks like you made a full recovery in a short time.* I wondered, *Does anyone ever make a full recovery?* I had not but somehow learned how to cope with my injury. I learned and successfully moved on. The experience of my stroke made me physically and mentally stronger, and at the end of the day, I came to believe it was a choice how I achieved recovery. It was essential to do things that helped my healing and growth, and I needed to get out there, try something new, and find what lit my *soul.*

Dear Self,

Emotions exist in your mind and heart. They change constantly. Never give up on yourself, no matter how hard life gets. Never turn to quick fixes because that won't help you in the long run. If you want to change yourself and grow, it will take time and small goals; before you know it, it will be weeks and months later. One year from now, you will look back and see how much you have grown. Every time you think of the moments that almost broke you, be proud and smile. Feel love for yourself. The sweet shortness of living brings us back to life—the existence of eternal love, joy, and bliss. There is no end to being; just go back to where your heart truly lives.

At some point in my recovery, I realized that grief was universal. Like many people, I experienced it through the death of a loved one, the loss of a job, the end of a relationship, and now the stroke. Grief was personal. Only I could really understand the pain. It wasn't neat or linear. It didn't follow predictable timelines or schedules. I cried, shouted, withdrew, and sometimes I just felt empty. I came to learn that none of this was unusual or wrong. One of my favourite poets is Rumi. He was a renowned writer, poet, and spiritual teacher who inspired me. He wanted people to wake up and see beauty in themselves and each other. Some say the universe is a mirror. If that is true, I have been the one creating my reality.

Don't grieve.
Anything you lose comes round in another form.

~Rumi

Dear Reader,

This is Your Gift of Grief

Why is it so difficult for us to let go of experiences that have caused pain and suffering? We get stuck in the past because of our need for certainty. We need to be assured that we can avoid pain and find some comfort in our lives. Letting go of the past also means stepping into the unknown. It means having the courage to be vulnerable and let go of what is familiar and learn from what's ahead, even if it feels negative. We need to embrace the unknown and the fear that lingers in our mind and heart.

Take some time for the self-reflection on the following pages to shift your mindset around grief.

Where Can I Find Gratitude Within Grief?

What Lessons Have I Learned About Grief?

What Part Of Grief Can I Release Control Of?

How Can I Accept Grief Right Now?

My Reflection Around Grief

My Poem About Grief

A Letter of Grief to Myself

Dear Self,

II

The Gift of Sorrow

My toes dangle bravely over dark edges
while my hands collect wishes that have forgotten how to shine.
You asked me...why do you want to be saved?
The truth is,
I think we all want to be held after we let go.
I think we all want to be saved with gentle words.

~Natasha Mochrie

During my second week in the hospital, I had daily visits with three neurologists, various nurses, and a few pharmacists. They all told me the same thing: I was going to be in the hospital for a long time. My parents asked me to think of some questions to help me with my recovery process. I said, *can I still have sex, and when? Can I ride my Harley? Can I still get tattoos?* My mother yelled at me for asking those questions, and my dad walked out of the room, regarding me like he believed the stroke didn't change a thing. My doctor said, considering my age, they were all valid questions.

The depression first appeared when I arrived at the trauma room five days later, unable to move my entire left side and possessing only one workable eye. It was extremely difficult to see my loved ones around me. Only their voices helped me identify them. I felt the depth of my grief as the doctor told me I might never walk again or obtain a normal view through my left eye. My sadness evolved into rage, despair, and depression: every negative emotion within me. *Why me?*

I lay in my bed and contemplated my suffering. I realized I accepted many false beliefs throughout my life. They told me that I needed to have lots of attachments, and my happiness was dependent on them. They were responsible for sowing the seeds of depression all around me. What was this depression? It was similar to grief. I felt lost, but I felt so much farther away from myself—hopeless. It was a sign I needed help and others to lean on.

In some ways, the depression was just a collection of thoughts: a series of false beliefs I learned from the beginning of childhood. I knew I wasn't destined to be plagued with depression. Instead, I could engage with it to transform myself. Although many negative emotions haunted me, I could live a life free of pain, jealousy, and fear if I could become conscious of my mind and thought processes. My depression was caused by a conviction that my negative thoughts were true; my despair was self-imposed.

As I navigated through my mind, I became aware of a rush of emotions. I was thinking about all the future situations that could occur, as well as the past struggles I needed to come to terms with. A focussed awareness of my feelings and responses allowed a transformation within me, helping to exhaust my suffering. I became free of the suffocation in my mind.

It would take time, but I soon became thankful I was alive and grateful for where life had brought me. It was a transition that made my inner self stronger. I decided to welcome any negative emotion that crept into my mind; I would open my heart and let in the fears, sadness, and anger. I would allow them to be. These were emotions that I had to experience in life, and I only learned to appreciate happiness when I genuinely recognized sorrow. There was always a way through adversity. I just needed to hold on. I would grow and become stronger through the darkest times.

Dear Mom,

As I write this, I'm not sure where my life will end up and why I am writing this at all. It's 1:00 in the morning, and I thought this was a better time to write you. During the day, I wear a mask of being okay, and at night I don't sleep at all. I'm listening to this band called Third Day, and the song is called Your Words. I think you and Dad should listen to it, and believe me when I say this to you, this is what I am feeling at this moment, and you'll understand why.

Mom, I believe a daughter's love for her mother never ends and will always carry over to the next life. My bond of love with you cannot be compared. These journal entries aren't easy to write, and I wonder why I keep needing to write them when I have technically "survived." I know I'm on the journey of recovery and living partially. The truth is, Mom, I don't see my future. I don't see myself giving up, but I also don't see myself fighting for this so-called life. I've always been good at reading situations and feeling things out, but I honestly feel like I am done with this part of my journey, even though my mind is screaming at me that I'm stronger than all of this.

Maybe my second chance is a way of me telling the people I love "thank you." Mom, I'm trying to find a way to say goodbye. I'm not sure if I can go on being trapped in this body and hurting anymore. This isn't easy, and I know life never is. There is so much I want to say, but I think my heart can only bear a little. Mom, I remember baking lemon pies in the cabin with you and when you held me,

19

singing *You Are My Sunshine*. I now sing that to Big Rigg. I'm not sure what age I was when we drifted apart, but I think I was a teenager. I know I broke your heart lots, Mom, and I'm sorry. I wish I had been better at times with the choices I made. I wish that we had spent more time together when I was younger, but I was so eager to grow up and see what life had to offer. This is probably hard for you to read, but I know that I will be okay, no matter where I end up. I'm smart and one hell of a fighter, but the fight inside me is withering.

When I had my stroke, it was a scary and difficult time. The worst part for me was it hurt you and Dad. I could see and feel your pain, and I thought I was a burden to you because I couldn't walk, let alone go to the bathroom by myself. The special time you and I had together in the hospital was so magical, and I felt so close to you; my favourite part was that you saw me get up and walk again—you saw the strength inside me. You were so proud. We sat in the dark and listened to my favourite music. After I first had my stroke, I didn't fight for myself. I fought for you and Dad because I didn't want to cause you more pain. Mom, I could go on for days about how much I love you and share all our memories, but I'm drifting to sleep. I know we're hours apart, but my love for you travels through the wind and tears and will hold us together until the next time I see you. Take care of yourself, Mom, and take care of Dad. I'll always be with you.

With love,
Your sunshine

Reflection...Save Tonight.

We sat under a sky full of stars, danced, spoke about life, and he asked me what I was grateful for. Everything that made me cry or knocked me down made me stronger in a way I am grateful for. I wouldn't be here in this moment and the woman I am if it were not for those experiences. He was astonished but managed to disguise it under his smile and warmth.

He said, Let the suffering be and allow your mind to let go.

Just like grief, there were stages in my emotions of sorrow, despair, and depression. I needed to be fully aware of them to reveal where I was broken and needed healing. In addition, I needed the care and support of people around me. I discovered that my negative thoughts and untrue beliefs were the sources of my unhappiness. If I could take control of my thoughts, emotions that seemed so powerful could not take over. Allowing the feelings to come and go on their own helped ease the pain and the problem; this was a natural process.

Releasing sadness and anger made me feel lighter. I learned that much of the emotional burden I carried stemmed from negative suppressed feelings and childhood traumas. They didn't define who I was. If my emotions could be fully allowed and embraced, healing would occur as a natural consequence. Well-being, positivity, and joy could be effortless. All I needed to do was let go. It was agony, but in the end, I felt almost invincible.

What hurts you, blesses you.
Darkness is your candle.

~Rumi

Dear Reader,

This is Your Gift of Sorrow

Healing is a return to wholeness, and healing from trauma is remembering that we can trust others, trust ourselves, and trust life. The calmness results from allowing life to be as it is rather than trying to control how it is perceived. It is not about waiting for others to initiate or sustain that connection, but rather, our willingness to try again, be vulnerable again, show up for others again, and reach out to be part of someone's life again. The most important part of healing is allowing ourselves to open up again. It is our willingness to show up as we are and trust that we will be taken care of, along with our discernment to give time and energy to those who respect and cherish the same. Finally, and most importantly, it is an awareness that, even though we all have to go through the fires of life, we can come out on the other end stronger and ready to appreciate what we have.

Take some time for the self-reflection on the following pages to shift your mindset around sorrow.

Where Can I Find Gratitude Within Sorrow?

What Lessons Have I Learned About Sorrow?

What Part Of Sorrow Can I Release Control Of?

How Can I Accept Sorrow Right Now?

My Reflection Around Sorrow

My Poem About Sorrow

A Letter To Myself About Sorrow

Dear Self,

III

The Gift of Resentment

It was the light from the moon,
the chill from the wind
as she swam around floating and
being fully surrounded by herself,
as she lay there so free of pain.

~Natasha Mochrie

I remember my sister, Chelsie, helping me one day. She is much smaller than I am, and she was trying to hold me up to dress me. Finally, I broke down and told her I couldn't feel the one side of my body. I felt like I was trapped and had nowhere to go. Everywhere I went, I wore sunglasses because the lights were too bright, and I wore noiseless headphones because I couldn't filter out loud sounds; they triggered headaches and seizures. Because my deficits weren't visible to everyone, people just stared at me.

Do I seem distracted and in distress? Would you prefer I speak in a more accommodating tone? Finding a way to express my emotions during the pain reduced my resentment. But I had to go back and look at the feelings that were turning my world upside down. I needed to visit the dark places where I was trapped.

What did it mean that I carried resentment? I suppose

because I was not happy with who I was, I blamed others. I blamed my friends and family, and it constantly blurred my self-image. There was nothing left in me to be confident about, nothing to help me claim what I loved about myself. How could I love myself? I was nothing but a disaster!

Over time, I realized I didn't forgive myself or anyone for the person I had become. When I looked at my family and friends, I saw people who experienced the freedom of healthy bodies and minds. There was no shadow hanging over them, so how could they even pretend that they understood what I was going through? I believed they only wanted to look socially acceptable by caring for me. What did they know? Everything about them was perfect. Look at me—the only miserable blot of pathetic imperfection in their gloriously perfect world.

Lying in a hospital bed, I cursed myself for being paralyzed and trapped in my own body. I was drowning as I repeatedly focussed on the condition of my physical body. No one taught me when I was a child that emotions could take on a physical personality. As a result, I never questioned whether or not emotions were like arms and legs capable of transporting me from one place in my psyche to another.

Contemplating about resentment helped me pull down some of the barriers I created. Why did my resentment make me so angry at others? It could completely take over my mind. I preserved the smallest infractions and stowed them greedily inside me. It became about my envy of their wholesome and perfect lives. In the end, I realized this was a poison to my mind, body, and soul.

Dear Dad,

Where do I even start? I love you, and I look up to you. I always have and always will, wherever I may end up. I am your brave daughter; I wish there was a pause button, so I could remember all the good times we had. When I fell, learning how to ride my bike, or when Mom got a picture of us trick-or-treating, I was your little devil; I had everyone and everything I ever needed. I learned how to make a fire and played outside, staring at the stars. I loved 4X4 in the truck with you, even when Mom and Chelsie were scared, and they sat at the bottom of the hill.

All those things made me strong and the spirited woman I am today. You taught me the importance of life; I went to nursing school because you told me always to help others, and I did my clinical aesthetics and now have my own business. Everything I have done is a reflection of you in some way. As I sit here listening to Tom Petty, "Free Falling," looking at Riggs and crying, I could probably write all night.

Dad, I can't tell you enough how much I love you. I'm a fighter, and that is a reflection of you. I always wanted to make you and mom proud; the stroke changed me, and I'm still fighting every day. Some days are worse than others, but they're shaping me into the person I really want to be deep down inside. I don't think I was fully living before; I was just letting life pass me by. Dad, this has been by far the hardest fork in my road, and I knew my life would change, but not this much. I don't want you to feel sorry for me. I love you, and I wish that I could know you'd be okay if I were to leave this sad, harsh world that we call home. I'm needed somewhere else. I will always be with you, and I'll always watch over you. I'll see you every time you look in the clear sky and the stars in the bright night. I love you; take care of yourself old man.

Like a serpent, resentment bit into my heart and rose through murky slime, blanketing all my senses, hissing in my head, seeping out of dark corners of my soul. I knew anger could lead to resentment, and these emotions began to take over my life.

Resentment felt like a physical thing. When it took hold of me, I became a different person. I believe emotions change and grow; they can bleed, they need nourishment, they multiply, and they can stimulate life or cause death. Yes, just like infected body tissue can kill, an infected emotion can do the same.

I know my resentment started with the anger I felt towards my friends and family: it led back to my anger at myself. Why did I ever have to experience a normal past only to lose it later on? Why did I ever have to walk and move as normal people do, only to lose the freedom of mobility? It would have been much easier to look at myself if I had always lived with the limitations of my injury. But that was not the case, and my past felt like a fantasy. My present looked so hopeless that the only version of myself I would accept as normal was the angry person who was authentic. One thing was clear: being angry at my past and resenting myself for once having a normal body meant I was creating obstacles while becoming the new me.

Reflection

Forgiveness is emancipation. If I cannot find my way to forgiveness, I will hold on to a harmful way of living. I cannot hold anyone responsible for my own mental and spiritual well-being. I hold this essential obligation to myself, and I forgive myself and others if we fall short. I must forgive and stop feeding the pain.

For me, the world was divided into those who wanted to benefit me and those who wanted to harm me. I needed to watch every step anyone took with me. I had to determine whether they were my friend or enemy before it was too late, and they got the better of me. This is what I constantly thought about the people in my life. And that is why I couldn't trust them. I knew I would continue to be mistrustful of everyone unless I could find a natural way to relax and stop distorting my vision of the people who were close to me. Not all my emotions were black and white. I needed to accept that situations arose, and people could not be categorized so harshly.

The candle that sparks,
the smell that eases the mood.
The soft touch of one's soul that breaks
each day for simply living
in rose-coloured glasses and
such a memory that
was never real.

~Natasha Mochrie

My anger would take over when I saw through people's politeness and attempts to control me and my expectations. *Are you being sarcastic when you tell me you understand how I feel? Are you patronizing me by telling me what you believe I can or cannot do? Don't try to explain what you meant because I'll be the judge of that.* This notion of myself stood in the way of reaching a consensus with my family. My pride had me in its clutches, and I had to pry my way out if I wanted to be at peace with others.

Some undesirable characteristics presented when I was resentful. Looking back on my time, trapped in that dark place,

I can explicitly relate to the person I was. How did I manage to grow out of that profile? Facing reality was one of the many gifts I gave myself. Reality was a much larger influence than what I thought about from a daily life perspective.

I really believe there is nothing like family. We are related to them by blood, and we expect them to be our closest allies. And yet, they strangely know nothing about who we truly are. They are supposed to be our greatest sources of love and support. However, our interactions with family are often filled with misunderstandings and resentment. Those who feel most like strangers often know a different version of us.

Yet, family is where our first and strongest emotional memories are made. Active awareness and empathy tell us how to respond to each other's needs. When we thoroughly know how we feel, we cannot be manipulated by someone else's emotions, nor can we blame our family conflicts for our choices.

At the lowest time during this experience, I felt abandoned by the people I needed the most. They didn't see the part of me that was evolving, healing, and discovering the real woman I was becoming. Deep down inside, though, I knew my family loved me and showed me their best version of support and wisdom.

After my debilitating stroke, it took a lot of time to overcome my resentment. My experience was painful. I was trapped inside a nightmare that I needed to wake up from. Unfortunately, I underestimated the message that reality was conveying to my soul. Although the mundane reality of who I used to be had undergone some changes, a new inner reality wanted to open up inside of me. It took the release of immense trauma, despair, and anguish for me to recognize this new reality.

Whoever I had become, the road to acceptance and forgiveness had changed me. When the gates swung out, I was led to a sublime realization of my destiny.

The truth is, unless you let go,
unless you forgive yourself,
unless you forgive the situation,
unless you realize that the situation is over,
you cannot move forward.

~Steve Maraboli

Dear Reader,

This is Your Gift of Resentment

We have an incredible amount of light in us. No matter the circumstances or where we are in life, we have the light that we can bring into our day at any moment we desire. We also have the choice to direct that light towards other people when we are compelled to. So even if something doesn't exactly go the way we planned, we can pause and smile at all the gifts we encompass. These gifts will shine on the frustration in our lives and the people around us. We really are unique and amazing beings, and it's time for us to start realizing that we can create lives filled with joy and fulfillment. We think it's the big moments and big shifts that change our lives forever, but it's the little realizations and daily thoughts that shape the lives we create for ourselves.

Take some time for the self-reflection on the following pages to shift your mindset around resentment.

Where Can I Find Gratitude Within Resentment?

What Lessons Have I Learned About Resentment?

What Part Of Resentment Can I Release Control Of?

How Can I Accept Resentment Right Now?

My Reflection Around Resentment

My Poem About Resentment

A Letter Of Resentment to Myself

Dear Self,

IV

The Gift of Fear

The pure elegance of quietness and beauty,
The ravishing,
The radiant,
The endless tears of sorrow,
The bright light in my dark...it was my clarity.

~Natasha Mochrie

The first year after the stroke marked a new stage of my recovery. The road was grueling, and the beginning was the most difficult. I had to face my greatest fears and deepest longings. Yet, looking back on those days, I can feel grateful now. I finally managed to reach a level of peace that stayed with me.

In the beginning, my nervous system was out of balance, and I had lost essential motor skills. It was hard for me to remember times and places. My ability to focus was gone, and my thoughts were scattered like candy spilled out of a jar. My brain struggled to restore its functioning. Multitasking was out of the question for me, and at intervals, a numbness would swell inside my head. The flexing mechanisms in my tendons and bones were in total shock. Basic motion was a monstrous challenge.

With each passing day, I became more hopeless. Struggling with balancing and walking tools exhausted me. Mentally and physically, I was in tatters, and there was nothing much I could do about it. Heavy fatigue always followed me like a shadow. It was cumbersome having to relearn all the basic skills I had performed as a child. In my search for something to ease my frustrations, I remembered that one of my favourite pastimes before my injury was keeping a journal. It gave me immense pleasure to record my thoughts and feelings on paper.

I remember feeling as if I was asking too much from people. Because I have always had a strong drive for independence, I never wanted the possibility that someone might judge me as being in need of too much help. In my heart, I understood that I had to learn to live differently from the way my friends lived and accept the sudden gulf between them and me; they were not striving for the same things. I could not deny that others' opinions were important while planning the life ahead of me, but I could not let others control me. My physical limitations forced me to face the contradiction that I still needed others. However, I had to make the right decisions for myself.

Eventually, I understood it was a waste of my time trying to explain my feelings and the jealousy I had of my friends' normal lives. That knowledge probably wouldn't have changed anything for them, and more importantly, I didn't need them to understand. Instead, I needed to confront my two most debilitating emotions.

For me, fear and doubt were different things. My doubts were disruptive negative thoughts about my capabilities and limitations. But fear was a dread of the future and not being able to live the life I wanted. Unlike my doubts, fear had the potential to be my friend; it urged caution and strategizing for the future. Fear made me aware of what needed to be done. Self-doubt told me I couldn't achieve it. Doubt kept undermining my efforts to move forward in my life. Making fear my friend woke me up—it showed me I could face the void that stood between me and my potential.

The shame of being a misfit tugged at me in the back of my mind, but I was slowly finding the strength to see myself as more than a prisoner in my body. I had gained a significant amount of weight while battling depression and being in a wheelchair. With my health further compromised, I had to face strengthening my body all over again.

The fear of being rejected by my intimate partner devastated me. I wanted to make an impression on him. He had once been special to me. Now, I doubted he would still want my companionship because of my physical impairment, and it was a doubt I was drowning in. In the early days, I was bitter and lacked faith in who I truly was.

Reflection

I had to learn the simplest things: walking again, multitasking, and cooking differently. The emotions I experienced were more complex than anyone could understand. The scariest part was learning how to have sex and intimacy again. I had to relearn those emotions and the comfort of physical touch. He told me that I was too vulnerable, saying the love I expressed was something out of a fairy tale.

If all the fears and doubts inside my broken soul were to be given a solid shape, they would form an immense landfill—layer upon layer of sediments, emotions, convictions, and suspicions—fears stacked upon doubts stacked upon fears. Stuck between those layers would be undeniable moments when I was certain I wanted to quit. The soil packing those landfilling layers included a past that accused my soul of all my negative emotions: anger, anxiety, loss, shame, and above all, fear and doubt.

Yet, those ingredients of my broken soul were strange things. They had power. They could teach truth like nothing else. There was no way of moving towards the life I yearned for without accepting that hope could crumble too soon, and it had to endure; those ingredients spurred me to grapple with greater truths. Fear and doubt became essential in telling me who I was; after discovering myself, I realized I was far more powerful than anyone had told me.

My revelations made me want to share the good news with everyone. An inner voice told me to hold on to myself; overcoming intense fear and doubt was possible, and there was a way to feel stronger and steadier. I could break out of the debilitating spell of doubt. Healing would take place in time—there was no shortcut or magic pill. Diligence, faith, and commitment were the only way forward through the states of fear and doubt. I needed time to come to terms with my present and forget about trying to retrieve my old life. I needed to accept the rebirth that shaped my future.

My mind had become a collection of puzzle pieces. It took an immense amount of patience to find the right places for them. The puzzle's shape had completely changed, and I had to figure out all the new places for each puzzle piece. I learned to conquer them one by one. My weakness turned into my ticket for happiness. I continued to face my fears and doubts, which helped me to convert my beliefs about my lack of abundance.

Over time, I realized I could pursue targets of larger significance, and I understood that consciousness and awareness worked at different levels. It was like a stairway climb up through a gloom-laden tower that surrounded me with cold walls blocking out the light. At first, while climbing through the dark, groping the dank walls, and staring up into the darkness, I could not make out anything. Then, as I continued on my upward path, I found the windows where the light could shine through. As I took another step, I peered through one window and then another; each new view gave me more perspective. I built on that perspective. I climbed higher because the guiding voice of faith told me there was more to see: a greater view was promised.

As I slowly started leaving my fears and doubts behind me, I realized I had a remorseless capacity to act as my own worst enemy. Sometimes I liked to throw a roadblock in my path to distract me from my fears and my deeper traumas. I had clung to those distractions like anchors of safety. Ultimately, however, that feeling of safety was an illusion, and my pretending simply became too exhausting otherwise.

When I finally let go of my self-doubts and fears about the future, I discovered I could walk out into the sunlight of warmth, compassion, and appreciation. These emotions were ready and waiting for me, and they lifted my soul, flowing like a waterfall of abundance. People in my life seemed kinder. I soon realized it was my responsibility to seek the higher perspectives that reflected the future I wanted. At long last, I felt grateful for my experiences and the person I was becoming.

You gain strength, courage, and confidence by every experience
in which you really stop to look fear in the face.
You are able to say to yourself,
"I have lived through this horror.
I can take the next thing that comes along."
You must do the thing you think you cannot do."

~Eleanor Roosevelt

Dear Reader,

This is Your Gift of Fear

Looking directly into the core of fear with solid stillness was once the only path to its absolute dissolution. However, added paths and big egos create more layers of illusion. Even though it may not seem too much at first, standing at the edge of an escarpment looking at a challenge ahead provides a pit in our stomach, and our breathing becomes faster and shallower; it's a feeling that can leave us frozen. How we choose to walk through it is up to us. We can either choose to succumb to the fear that freezes us, or we can process an emotion like uncertainty in order to flip our outlook.

Take some time for the self-reflection on the following pages to shift your mindset around fear.

Where Can I Find Gratitude Within Fear?

What Lessons Have I Learned About Fear?

.

What Part Of Fear Can I Release Control Of?

How Can I Accept Fear Right Now?

My Reflection Around Fear

My Poem About Fear

A Letter Of Fear To Myself

Dear Self,

V

The Gift of Transition

Mirror, mirror, in the sky,
What is it actually like to fly?
To only go into the abyss of the unknown?
I am brave, I am strong.
I am a pathway of light from my hallowed heart.

~Natasha Mochrie

Accepting the realities of my new life appeared to be a simple task. However, like most people, I had my own filters for reality. Some of them were based on regret, disappointment, and denial while others were dependent on me simply waiting for something better to come along. I had pants in my wardrobe that hadn't fit in years because I wasn't accepting a part of my reality. The new me couldn't change without me putting forth any effort.

Changing myself meant giving up false versions of my life. Honestly facing situations was the first step towards improving them. It took a lot of resilience to transform my life, and there were some tough hurdles to manage. Even positive life events during my recovery disrupted my long-established habits.

I woke up to an unpredictable world every day. Without my old routines, I was thrown off balance, and new situations tested my coping abilities. When I looked at myself, I realized what had once appeared a remote possibility, was now my reality. I thought, *when people talk about the new normal, maybe they are referring to this.* My life had changed, but it no longer carried the weight of despair. I experienced the sense of a new beginning!

It's possible that some of my *new normal* included things I had always feared yet equally desired. Otherwise, they were just too ordinary to notice. Even if I didn't like my new reality, accepting it was necessary for me to move on with living.

Dear Self,

What are these memories standing out for me: being in a wheelchair, using a walker, relying on a cane, then limping back and forth to the mailbox? Is this how I see my new reality and how I measure getting better?

How do I know where to start? Determine where you want to be in your life. Take a look at what's changed. Be truthful with yourself about what you enjoy and don't like about your new existence. Observe all the differences evolving over time, and focus on the small, immediate experiences. This is the start of your new life. This is the new normal for you. Only the present moment is true.

What is important about what I left behind? Bid farewell to your previous self, but do not dismiss it completely. Remember all the wonderful and unremarkable things that you moved through. Give your past a special place in your memory and accept that this is no longer who you are.

What is my new life rhythm? Your new normal has a different beat. Take advantage of the opportunity to create and implement your unique new routines. In your new reality, you can be assertive. You have the ability to reclaim control over your life. Be open to new experiences that will shape your future. Even if it feels scary, try to explore something new. Your life rhythms are reflections of who you are now.

What about what's missing? As you settle into your new routine, take note of what's lacking. Allow time to grieve if you find yourself longing for the past. If you still miss experiences or people from your old life, come up with strategies to invite them back in. Create an invitation for wholeness in your life.

What is emerging? Consciously notice and welcome new experiences and relationships that emerge as you adjust to your new normal. This includes the newly-developed personal relationship with yourself. You're always changing and evolving as a person, and eventually, you will be able to accept, and even embrace, your new identity.

As a child, I knew I was loved by my family and friends, and I had everything I needed: a roof over my head and healthy food in my belly. And yet, I found it tough in some ways. I was closer with my grandparents than my parents due to spending more time at their home than at my own. My grandparents never missed a play, recital, or special achievement of mine.

My papa was my strength, and I always looked up to him. He called me his Queen of the Nile because I wore bright blue eyeshadow, and he told me my sassiness and fire would inspire many. He passed away on the day before my 30th birthday, and I'll always remember him as the lighthouse that led me home.

Major changes occurred as I progressed through life. My daily routine changed, right down to the moment I first opened my eyes. Sometimes, it was hard to adjust to my new routine, and I realized something profound—aging is a major life-altering event in and of itself. Accepting change was essential for my personal development and happiness. And accepting change as the only constant was liberating.

I didn't know where evolution would take me, but I considered that being human meant there was a possibility I could reach my full potential. Life became about reinventing myself, and reinvention wasn't just about pursuing pleasure or achievement. I knew there was a distinction between being aware of who I am as an authentic individual versus just experiencing its rewards. After winning the prize, I knew I wasn't done. But this wasn't the whole story anymore.

Reinvention sprouted endless, mostly positive opportunities. It gave me the freedom to continue discovering new aspects of myself. Exploration was growth, and this growth was inward-looking rather than outward-looking. I realized I had the means to reinvent myself whenever I discovered something I wanted to change.

Dear Self,

See yourself from the outside. Consider yourself a sculptor. A sculptor stares at a block of stone and wonders about new ways to shape it. There is no emotional bias when he thinks about how he will modify it. Just go ahead. This is how to see yourself: as a work of art that is constantly evolving. When you see something you don't like, there's no need to get frustrated with or harsh towards yourself. Instead, get to work like an artist would.

Find the habits that support the changes you want to make. Far too often, you tend to focus on the visible problems rather than the habits that created the problem in the first place. For example, you tried to overcome being overweight by performing a lot of workouts rather than admitting that part of the problem was a poor diet.

To fully reinvent yourself, you had to identify the behavior that gave rise to the trait in the first place and then make the necessary adjustments.

You gained a significant amount of weight due to depression, being in a wheelchair for months and not having any type of appetite except for protein shakes. All you did was sit in meditation: practice, practice, practice. Change wasn't something you could implement on certain days and abandon on others. Instead, you realized that transition encompassed daily commitment to the point that new habits replaced old ones and no longer required a conscious effort.

Set realistic goals. You can't suddenly decide one day that you aren't going to be impatient. You are correct to assume that won't occur spontaneously, and you are actually helping yourself by admitting that a nasty habit won't go away overnight. Instead, make it a mission to be more patient during frustrating times. Use it as a private practice and reminder of what you want to work on.

Surround yourself with honest people. It is unlikely that everyone you know will agree with your choices. You need people who will question and challenge you. You need folks who aren't scared to tell it like it is. Tough but honest feedback is necessary for your personal development, and then, you can decide for yourself.

You have to take risks. If you continue being the person you are now, you will never be the person you want to become. Change is the only normal, not simply the new one. The only thing growth asks is that you leave your comfort zone—that is all there is to it. And until you're willing to take that step into the unknown, you'll always be stuck where you are. It's an art to reinvent yourself. It's also a process, not a short-term treatment or an overnight fix. Personal evolution is a required day-in, day-out, conscious practice that supports you to invent who you want to be.

Look at yourself in the mirror. When you refuse to stop and take a good look at yourself, things can go off course and become deadly if you avoid self-reflection. There's a time and place for that go, go, go mode, but there's also a time and place to slow down and contemplate. You'll quickly discover that unless you take the time to ask yourself the tough questions, you'll lose where you've been and have no idea how you got here.

There were times when it was really hard to look at myself in the mirror. I just couldn't see the person who I used to be. I was sad to lose her, but that wasn't the only issue; the woman staring back at me was not the person I was meant to become. The better version of me was yet to arrive.

You are not the person you used to be.
Don't be afraid to tell people you have changed.
Your boundaries look different. Your outlook looks different.
You're not tolerating what you used to.
You are walking on a path of purpose and conviction.
Reintroduce yourself so they get to know the new you.

~Ash Alves

Dear Reader,

This is Your Gift of Transition

Establishing a few daily disciplines starts a whole new life process. Consistency is the key. We must never let good be the enemy of great and never let what we cannot do stop us from doing what we can. We won't always feel motivated, but we need to push past it. Discipline is doing what needs to be done, especially when we weren't initially excited to do it. Anyone can work hard when motivated, but to be consistent, we must push ourselves when we aren't inspired. Our greatest strength as human beings is our ability to transform ourselves. Self-discipline is the foundation upon which all good habits are built. Self-discipline is the ability to do what you know you should when temptation whispers in your ear. It is like courage; we are born with it. And we develop it further by taking action despite how we feel. When we act courageously, it doesn't mean we aren't experiencing trepidation. It means we took action despite our fear.

Take some time for the self-reflection on the following pages to shift your mindset around transition.

Where Can I Find Gratitude Within Transition?

What Lessons Have I Learned About Transition?

What Part Of Transition Can I Release Control Of?

How Can I Accept Transition Right Now?

My Reflection Around Transition

My Poem About Transition

A Letter Of Transition to Myself

Dear Self,

VI

The Gift of Limbo

Papa,
Like a lighthouse, you shine the brightest in the darkest hours.
Your light is never dull for those who seek it.

~Natasha Mochrie

Accepting the realities of my new life was a beginning. However, after I crossed the thresholds of doubt and fear, I passed into a place that felt like nothingness. There was an impenetrable silence that surrounded me. Somewhere on my journey through recovery, I discovered *the void*. This limbo stage seemed like nothingness, yet it had a tangible presence. It was a place I had to reside in before moving on, and it appeared to have no end. Now I would face the full impact of my numbness.

I considered the many experiences that wouldn't have happened if not for the stroke. It felt like I was going through different stages, with several presenting themselves since my becoming incapacitated by the stroke. Of all of them, limbo was the most desolate. I could feel nothing, not even despair. I forgot what it was to love or care about anything. I was numb to my core, realizing it was unbearable; death seemed preferable to an existence of feeling nothing. I knew I had to find the will and the means to escape this limbo, but I still couldn't understand why the stroke had happened. Soon, why it happened was no longer critical. Everything afterwards is what really changed me.

Reflection

I am standing at the edge of a forest and gazing up; I see a wall of trunks and treetops. Fear tugs at my consciousness because I know I have to enter the dense growth, but my steps take me into secret crawlspaces deep beneath those formidable trunks. As I try to slow my racing heart, I crawl one step after another until emerging into a clearing. A little farther, there is a pool. I walk down to its edge and stare into the water. The water is clear and still. I see my face looking up at me, and then, without knowing what is happening, my consciousness is pulled under the watery surface. I am suddenly in limbo where everything is as still as death.

Fear encompassed me as I walked through the dense wood. Making my way through the prickly shrubs and looming corpses of my thoughts, I confronted self-doubt. But within this state of stillness, I was filled with dreaded emptiness. The nothingness is vividly absolute, and its breath is overwhelmingly hot on my face. It leers at me and juts out its finger to touch the center of my consciousness.

I knew I was experiencing something profound in this looming void, having been afraid many times before when it crept into my soul. However, I had never experienced anything like this presence, and I had no emotion to anchor me. Being aware of the void inside me made me realize that my place within this new terrain was unique. It was evident when it opened up, holding itself in place, neither shrinking nor growing. The black emptiness was like a midnight sun, an interstellar black hole that kept staring back at me.

What did this mean? I was a thing held among all other things in the vastness of the universe. I recognized the possibility of simultaneously existing and not existing, with each cancelling the other out. At that moment, my rational mind was overwhelmed, and my ego was left, considering the randomness and unimportance of my existence.

I was in the stillness of a vacuum—no moving right, no moving left, no going forward or backward. Depression was easier to comprehend because it was in motion, like a plotline unfolding, showing various stages through which it evolved. On the other hand, the void was unfeeling, unmoving, and unchanging. It overtook my consciousness, absorbing every piece of me until I was only aware of the emptiness that enveloped me.

Everything I had believed about myself was no longer valid, and all the identities that previously gave meaning to my life were nullified. I no longer had an identity. This was limbo. The void gave me the experience of standing in the great unknown, confronting who I really was and why I was here. Moreover, questions arose about what it meant to have a relationship with anyone. Or did they all lack meaning? They began to seem like illusions. When I finally accepted that I did not have any answers to my nagging questions, I surrendered to understanding nothing.

After the stroke, I started imagining situations as excerpts from a mental health textbook. In this scenario: *Natasha had a life-altering experience. She went from being stuck in a rut, to having an unwanted life transition, to experiencing a crisis, to losing her identity, to losing someone she loved. Administer medications and watch for signs of depression.*

It was a severe challenge for me to cope with my state of uncertainty. Finding out that I didn't know the answers to the most basic questions about my existence was one thing. However, accepting that it wasn't possible to answer those questions was another. Over time, I figured out that I couldn't find the answers to my questions by walking down an aisle at the grocery store or skimming through my wardrobe for something to wear for my evening date. Instead, I had to do some deep reflection to discover the root of my confusion.

Maybe I had nothing better to do besides thinking about the reasons for my existence. But I seemed to have an abundance of time to wonder about the meaning behind everything happening to me. I was confident there was a new vitality inside my impaired body, so the impulse of life buried deep inside my soul slowly achieved new meaning while discarding old forms and interpretations. Life gave me a chance to go deeper, and as a result, I came to understand that joy accompanied my starkest moment of psychological death. While standing in my limbo, I witnessed a deadly global pandemic pushing everyone into their version of limbo, and I simultaneously saw myself moving towards the power I needed for my release.

Reflection

The day I had my stroke, a massive part of me died. I now realize I could no longer be who I was previously because I was destined to fulfill a greater purpose. The first step was accepting that reality did not provide definite answers. My reality was more significant than what I observed through the lens of a mundane world. I gradually understood the words of psychologist Maurice Joseph:

> *We're born into a world of things unknown,*
> *but with minds that don't like to tolerate that.*

I learned how to tolerate the questions the void posed for me. During my experience being in limbo, I found a precariously thin line between accepting and rejecting my walk into the unknown. If I had chosen rejection at that time, I would not be sharing my story in this memoir. Likewise, I would not have discovered the values that matter the most.

During those days, it made a big difference to have a sense of community that included people who could accept me as I was and on my terms. The numbness was overcome through people's gestures of kindness and the intimate conversations they offered. Besides a community of support, I committed to other values that supported me to create a new outlook— moving on from limbo required embracing kindness, respect, honesty, knowledge, compassion, and abundance—for myself and others. A sense of community reminded me what a tremendous gift it was to have someone to connect with when the void opened up inside me. I realized that sharing the pain within my life story created the connection to the community that I craved.

Meditation practice guided me the most through the process of limbo. It was ironic to learn that many philosophies deeply recognized the void as a spiritual experience. This had mental, emotional, and physical implications for me. Eventually, the void allowed me to surrender control and regain wholeness, balance, and clarity during meditation. When I was unaware, questions surfaced that focused on the past and future. However, meditation allowed me to shut out past and future thoughts and concentrate on the present. As a result, being immediately present was an experience of the void that needed nothing more.

I gradually wore out the doubts that arose from my failures by letting go of my past. Likewise, releasing the future allowed my consciousness to slowly unmoor itself from constant worry about what was to come. It was remarkable to discover that, while

I was constantly encouraging myself to focus on the present, I could free myself from my obsessions about consequences. I left behind the provinces of reward, punishment, success, and misfortune.

In the end, I was left with my raw self, having looked the void in the eye and somehow acquired the essence of the here and now. I chose to let go of the burden of emotions originating from the past and the future. I was stripped naked by the void, which revealed my essential self.

Anyone can achieve their fullest potential.
Who we are might be predetermined,
but the path we follow is always of our own choosing.
We should never allow our fears or the expectations of others
to set the frontiers of our destiny.
Your destiny can't be changed but it can be challenged.
Every man is born as many men and dies as a single one.

~Heidegger

Dear Reader,

This is Your Gift of Limbo

There are times in our lives when everything is going smoothly, and then, we suddenly run into a gust of wind that topples us over. It may feel like life is throwing us a curveball from out of nowhere. When we find ourselves wanting to throw in the towel, it's important to pay close attention to our internal selves.

Take some time for the self-reflection on the following pages to shift your mindset around limbo.

Where Can I Find Gratitude Within Limbo?

What Lessons Have I Learned About Limbo?

What Part Of Limbo Can I Release Control Of?

How Can I Accept Limbo Right Now?

My Reflection Around Limbo

My Poem About Limbo

A Letter To Myself About Limbo

Dear Self,

VII

The Gift of Wisdom

Save Tonight.
Thank you for showing me a love I've never felt
and helping me see life as it really is.
We've had a short time together.
For the very first time in my life,
I felt loved and wanted in a mindful, intimate way.
You showed me how to take life less seriously
and treasure the present time
because some things won't last, and we have only
this one chance at life.
Thank you for showing me a more authentic image of myself
and the woman I can become.
The love I had for you made me a better person.

~Natasha Mochrie

When I considered my life experiences, I discovered two different worlds: my inner and outer realities. The external world played out events like scenes on a giant movie screen. I saw myself and all the characters on it trying to agree on whom I was supposed to be. I did my best to conform. However, I couldn't lie to myself in my inner world. I have always known I wasn't the best of learners as a child. It wasn't a lack of intelligence; I just had little interest in what educators taught us. Often, it was difficult because there were huge differences between my inner reality and what people thought was happening to me in the outside world.

I spent most of my life focussing on my inner development. I didn't know if that was good for me. I felt compelled to delve into myself where questions pushed their way to the surface. I believe some people climb the tallest mountains in the world, and when they're near the top, clinging to the rock face, they know they have found themselves. Others discover their purpose when they look into the eyes of their firstborn child. Many people strive to achieve success by following their business instincts and pushing themselves to their peak potential. I found myself asking more profound questions and pushing my ego to its limits to obtain understanding.

Even with both eyes closed,
my heart couldn't find a way to unlove you.

~Wilder

In my situation, I recognized I needed to be single-minded and willing to give up almost anything to find myself again. Some things were easy to give up; most physical activities were ruled out while confined to my bed. Peace of mind was not easy to attain. I had been left in a state of confusion after coming through a crushing experience. I felt like I had more ground to cover than most people because of my particular debilitation. I didn't believe my journey was necessarily more challenging than others, but my experience of the stroke was unique.

Reflecting on my childhood, the opposing realities of my inner and outer life were undeniable during my educational experiences. My dad and mom always told me I was bright and capable at school. Certain teachers thought I could excel if

I put in a little more effort. I couldn't process what I felt when I heard those words from my parents and teachers. Perhaps I was made complacent by such compliments, merely satisfied in knowing I was capable of achieving. Whatever the case, I never felt motivated to learn through the traditional education system. It didn't seem to recognize what I needed. I wonder what kind of difference in my life it would have made if my parents and teachers had just asked me why and what made me unique?

Something told me that the lessons taught in school had little to do with the way life was. This settled the matter of my disinterest. I had different emotional needs from those who obediently wrote their exercises and patted themselves on the back for doing it. I instinctively wanted to experience more. I needed more. My school was boring. My mind wanted to go beyond the constant limitations. Before too long, I realized that life was not what the school system promised me. The events in my life that could have benefited from education were situations not listed anywhere in my textbooks.

While my classmates were busy defining themselves by their performance at school, I was busy wanting to find out about sex, relationships, mindfulness, and the true nature of human beings. I explored viewpoints about specific causes, why we loved and hated, how much psychology understood people, and the different ways we interpreted ourselves. I was a student philosopher.

I wish educators spent more time teaching children emotional literacy. Many people I know are skilled at keeping their jobs but cannot manage their emotions in intimate relationships. I came to believe that when couples or families run into arguments, they mess things up because they don't have the language for emotions; they need to learn to connect with their feelings and express them authentically.

The education process at school was terribly out of sync with my unique needs and opportunities. However, I never gave up on the idea of advancing my education. My parents taught me early on that schooling was indispensable. Eventually, I discovered hope through a new approach to learning.

My rebel mind endured its struggles with organized education. My heart lamented the confinement imposed on people like myself; there were consequences to the traditionally limited systems in education at the time. From the perspective of the mystic, the inner and outer worlds overlapped. The truth was not a caged bird on display, bound and claimed by one person or group. It was a bird that stopped to perch on a branch to give its wings a break and sing a song. It would soar again. Borders do not stop truth on its journey.

Out beyond ideas of wrongdoing
and right-doing, there is a field.
I'll meet you there.
When the soul lies down in that grass
The world is too full to talk about.
Ideas, language, even the phrase each other
Doesn't make any sense.

~Rumi

After confronting my spiralling fears and doubts and surviving through the void, I stepped through the door of renewal. Now was the time to look towards education to help empower the new person I had become. I wasn't just a new body; I had a new way of operating, and my whole outlook had changed.

Every nuance of my new body's movements made me

realize I had to begin by accepting myself. The first thing I wanted was to rediscover beauty. I needed to examine and redefine what it meant to me; I craved the chance to sense once again that the outside world could be beautiful. I wanted to see beauty in places that would give me a sense of awe. From the beginning, self-education would help me realize my goals.

In my initial planning, I considered how many people rely on formal education to establish their careers. Most of us do it out of necessity. We promote academics and formalized education to create qualified practitioners in particular professions. Pursuing self-learning helped me explore my passions and many non-traditional schools of knowledge. Self-learning required a lot of discipline because I was on my own, and there was no one else to ensure I was being responsible. The only person I had to answer to was myself, and I was motivated to work that much harder.

Although I knew I could teach myself new skills and gain knowledge, I wasn't always confident about my learning capacity since the stroke. However, I was hungry for transformation. I realized that I had one chance at life. That was enough to conquer the fear of trying different things. My self-education plans offered a clean slate to the gift of learning.

I loved learning on my own because I quickly developed my skills at releasing negative thoughts and patterns. By choosing to learn new things, I changed my daily routines to remove the obstacles holding me back. Life learning would never end for me, as I could always imagine a better version of myself. Once, an epiphany came to me while I was sitting in a room full of individuals and realized that we had unique learning and emotional needs; education wasn't going to reach all of us. I needed to find my own way.

In some ways, writing this book was part of my education

and growth. There was a particular lesson for me discovering my inner strength and allowing myself to receive it fully. The inexplicable, tragic accident I experienced had left me in a dark place. New learning was a fire to light up in that darkness. I began to read books on success, motivation, and the lives of people who created businesses that transformed them on the path to manifestation. Love and gratitude guided me, and I discovered lessons that resonated with me. I made new pieces to fit my transforming self.

Your task is not to seek for love
but merely to seek and find all the barriers within yourself
that you have built against it.

~Rumi

Life itself had become my true educator: life and love. I was raised with the self-limiting belief that there was no connection between my inner reality and the outside world. As I read the concepts that inspired me, I severed myself from those limiting beliefs. Lifelong learning facilitated personal evolution. Perhaps a perfectly integrated system didn't exist, but growth was a necessary path for personal fulfilment. The constant thirst for knowledge kept me running towards different goals in my life. It helped engage my mind and body to pursue experience and happiness. It raised the bar for myself and my standards of living. Formal and non-formal education, combined with a personal growth mindset, created significant advantages. As a lifelong learner, I feel healthier and happier, and I'm convinced I will live longer.

Dear Self,

Set daily goals: *Decide how much free time you have. Set aside a portion each day for self-learning, perhaps half an hour or longer. This time is for self-education only. Find learning materials that interest you.*

Practice journaling: *Write your thoughts down and observe your self-expression. Notice any themes and feelings about them. Notice anything interesting. Do this every day.*

Create challenges that lead to growth: *They are necessary for your personal development if you wish to move forward. You can only achieve a fraction of your true potential while living a too-comfortable life. Comfort zones can become lethal barriers to stagnation. They can represent a resistance to change and discourage you from rising to the occasion or pursuing excellence. Sometimes, reaching the end of a path means hiking a long way, uphill. When the challenge appears too big, take smaller steps.*

Embrace the growing pain: *Each challenge you overcome leads to personal growth. This process will boost your confidence level, and you can learn to trust in yourself more the next time. Remember the first day you could have a shower and shave without someone holding you up and how you felt like a woman again.*

Seek inner satisfaction and pleasure: *Overcoming challenges reveal your capacity to experience joy and fulfillment. Choose small challenges and celebrate as you accomplish them. Notice every milestone you pass. The more you achieve your goals, the more you will see that the only limitations came from your imagination. Find happiness in small moments.*

Never underestimate the power of dreams
and the influence of the human spirit.
We are all the same in this notion:
The potential for greatness lives within each of us.

~Wilma Rudolph

Dear Reader,

This is Your Gift of Wisdom

Sometimes the key to finding joy and success is not focusing on the big picture but on the little moments that make up our daily life. Some of the best things in life are found in the beauty and joy of precious moments that fill our lives with meaning and happiness. Creating a compelling vision of our future but concentrating on the many small steps it takes to achieve our goal while pausing to notice the little moments along the way can help us obtain the most out of the present. When we feel tired and frustrated, it is possible we are focussing too much on the big picture—try to pause to enjoy beauty and life's little pleasures—the frost on your windshield or an unexpected compliment. Attention to detail has the added benefit of positively impacting performance and leading to increased success. By focussing on the *small stuff*, we achieve improvement that builds long-term goals. Focusing on the little things and taking baby steps forward creates progress and improves our daily lives.

Take some time for the self-reflection on the following pages to shift your mindset around wisdom.

Where Can I Find Gratitude Within Wisdom?

What Lessons Have I Learned About Wisdom?

What Part Of Wisdom Can I Release Control Of?

How Can I Accept Wisdom Right Now?

My Reflection Around Wisdom

My Poem About Wisdom

A Letter To Myself About Wisdom

Dear Self,

VIII

The Gift of Attachment

Love
Like the clear glass lake, we floated on through
the most incredible summer.
That summer and present time will always
follow the line of least resistance.
If you must force the path of the unknown,
it's truly not meant for you.
There comes a point when everyone of us questions
whether love is truly worth all the pain and the loss.
The answer will always be yes.
Yes, to the moments and people who make you fall and let go.

~Natasha Mochrie

The best part of my recovery arrived with a new understanding of my spiritual reality. According to some spiritual traditions, I was already an aware and fully conscious being. With all my perceived limitations and strivings, my highest self existed in a state of perfection. The eternal part of me was not affected by things, people, or events that might trigger me. My ego was the part of myself that sometimes snuck up on me and made me believe I was only a flawed human being.

Attachment is a concept in Buddhism that helped me understand my relationship with the outside world. I knew that I was attached to so many things: my home, my family, my identity. I loved my dog, Bigg Rigg, like nothing else in the world, and I couldn't bear to think of losing him. Being attached to things wasn't necessarily wrong. But my grasping onto them and refusing to let them go could be, especially when that was necessary for my growth. I started to imagine what it would be like if I were less attached to material things. It was a spiritual discipline to have a certain detachment from external rewards. It wasn't a lack of love or compassion towards others, and in fact, I felt closer than ever when I realized how easy it was to lose them. I hoped I would find a way to quiet the noise in my head and achieve a state of peace.

Reflection
March 19, 2020
11:11 PM

As I lie awake here drowning in my thoughts, I wonder why I'm alive and if it matters. What is my purpose for living? Suddenly, I feel brave, but I cry myself to sleep. I dream that I repeatedly tell myself that I will walk this path with strength and dignity, and I will live graciously no matter my outcome. Someone once told me that "one day love would set me free." I discovered those words to be immaculately true: my biggest strength is the love I have for myself.

As I learned more about my emotional attachments, I started to understand how feelings of affection and closeness defined meaningful relationships. My earliest bonds were formed with my parents and family members. Those experiences of attachment shaped all future attachments, including friendships and romantic relationships. I learned that having secure attachments to others helped people develop a sense of connection to social groups and communities. Healthy connections allowed me to feel happy and safe: they played a crucial role in my experience of belonging.

I understood that intimate relationships could be complicated, from the initial physical attraction to courtship and meaningful commitment. My partners and I each came to the table with our baggage. I knew that emotional attachments were sometimes intense and could even lead to dependency and impact my well-being, but how would I know if I was too attached?

Detachment required my practice of mindfulness and took me almost two years of shadow work, three journals, countless hours of meditation, and the processing of much sorrow. Slowly, however, I started to realize how crucial it was to experience a sense of well-being based on nothing more than my awareness and being present in my body. Detachment helped me understand that it was ok to sometimes distance myself from the world, materialistic things, and the people who no longer brought positive influences into my life. I couldn't allow my sense of self to be emotionally swayed by people, outside events, or even my limited perceptions and thoughts. I would be forever caught cycling between joy and sorrow. It was necessary to let go of my expectations of others.

Living mindfully and being more detached from outward achievements allowed me to relate to people and things with appreciation. I felt purpose in trying to enjoy my life by any means possible. Happiness was no longer defined and controlled by something outside of me; my mind was set free. By practising mindfulness, I could achieve some distance in my relationships. Love could be pure and present at the same time. Two years prior, there was a man who I truly loved and who captured a part of me I didn't know existed. The time we spent together transformed me. In the end, he didn't have the same feelings towards me, so I knew we had a short time together; living in the present helped me treasure every moment. Since then, I have chosen to do everything with love in my heart and presence because I know my time spent with loved ones will never last as long as I want it to.

The Importance of Detaching

Dear Self,

Throughout your life, you will have to face decisions about holding onto things or letting them go. It will be one of your greatest challenges, but you'll learn that you need to let go to move forward. Sometimes it's impossible to hold on to what we desire most; these will be ideas about truth, objects of importance, and all kinds of relationships. It might be painful to lose them. As a human, you were conditioned to hold onto things, and the thought of abandoning them was too much to bear. You can take a step back and look beyond letting go. It might be difficult, but that future place offers something, perhaps a new opportunity waiting for you.

Sometimes, you will feel incomplete and insecure whenever you think about releasing something. You'll imagine it will be hard to replace what you've lost. Ask yourself if what you have right now is good for you. If there is a shred of doubt, determine what is most important to keep in your life, no matter who or what the situation is. You create your destiny. Pay attention and take control of your fate. Move towards growth. As you grow, you'll evaluate what you need and decide to try new things and determine what brings you happiness and fulfilment. You need to be honest with yourself. It may be hard to let go at first. However, you will start to adapt.

Things will get easier. You will look back upon what you left behind and see that you moved forward. Work towards self-development. Imagine new opportunities. You can choose to be hopeful and expect good things are on the way if you strive for them.

In the past, you discovered how negative emotions and thoughts affected you and why it was essential to let go of them. You had to identify the feelings and thoughts that needed to be released. What needs to be cleared from your psyche now? Remember to let go of anything that does not serve a positive intention. These might be events and emotions from the past when you didn't experience desired outcomes. Let go of old sorrows, doubts, and fears that are holding you back.

Remember that choosing not to move forward won't bring someone back. Holding on to their memory can lead to unnecessary pain and disturb the balance needed in your mental, emotional, and physical states. This can prevent you from enjoying life to the fullest and exploring hopeful, new possibilities. Accept what is unchangeable, face a new reality, and move on. Once you have moved on successfully, you'll learn to appreciate your evolution from experience and see the roads leading to a new future. Learn to live life in the moment and understand that uncertainty is the only constant in life. Life is beautiful all the same.

True detachment is not a separation from life,
but the absolute freedom within your mind to explore living.

~Ron W. Rathbun

Dear Reader,

This is Your Gift of Attachment

There is so much shame around endings. And things are important. Without an ending we don't have a beginning. We are not a quitters, failures, or losers for ending anything that doesn't serve a purpose. Many of us stay in an unhealthy situation for too long because we're afraid of what people might think. You might be judged by others. Some people are going to say things about us no matter what, so we might as well do what makes us happy and content.

Take some time for the self-reflection on the following pages to shift your mindset around attachment.

Where Can I Find Gratitude Within Attachment?

What Lessons Have I Learned About Attachment?

What Part Of Attachment Can I Release Control Of?

How Can I Accept Attachment Right Now?

My Reflection Around Attachment

My Poem About Attachment

A Letter To Myself About Attachment

Dear Self,

IX

The Gift of Peace

When you almost die, you realize that every moment,
every minute counts because it could be your last.
So, if you fall, then fall hard but make sure you get up,
and if you cry, shed those tears but then wipe them away.
Always remember you are alive,
and you are an incredible individual.
Take in those deep breaths and slow thoughts,
and feel the warmth of every word left upon your soft lips.
Save Tonight.

~Natasha Mochrie

Finding peace within myself was always an internal journey; it was up to me to forgive myself. I remembered the first time I asked, *does anyone ever become fully healed?* Perhaps the word healing was misunderstood because it implied that I no longer had pain, that I no longer thought about the hurt or how little I was left with. I saw healing differently. Strangely, I doubted I could ever be fully recovered, but I discovered peace and moved my life forward anyway. I'll always have a memory of loss, and I'll always have my doubts. I'll have to face them honestly and learn to accept them.

If I were given a choice and told that the stroke and healing process would help me evolve to my potential and make me a better person, I would choose the path of growth.

Those experiences helped me get in touch with my life's most important questions and helped me realize who I was as a soul beyond my personality and body. They helped me to appreciate love and life's sacred moments of beauty.

Part of finding peace within myself was understanding more about the healing process. There were differences between physical and emotional recovery. Much of my mental and emotional life was challenging to treat, and the injury was unclear. Recovery depended on so many individual factors that there was no standard for everyone; we all developed and healed differently. Do you ever recover from losing the love of your life? Or do you just learn to move on because you don't want to be left behind?

I found peace within myself when I decided I no longer wanted to stay in the place I was mentally and physically. I became so aware of my emotions and thoughts that any negativity that came into my life, whether from past relationships or friends, was quickly left behind. Anything that was not meant for my divine purpose was brushed aside. By consciously choosing to move forward, I realized I had taken the most crucial step in my healing process. Peace flowed within me and shaped events in my outer world. It occurred to me that this possibility was available to everyone.

While I may not have fully healed, I have learned to become more than healing emotions. My healing experiences led me through various stages, and I became more aware of my spiritual nature. I started to have my spiritual awakening. I awoke from my mind and surroundings that had been clouded for the longest time. As I proceeded mindfully through my healing process, I started to see the part of myself that was more than my thoughts.

Reflection

It was my first taste, the one I was craving, like being so thirsty and experiencing the second the water hit my lips and tongue. It was the toe-curling, the eye connecting, and the lip-biting—that fuzzy feeling running inside me. It's what I lived for; it's what I wanted more of; it's what I felt like as he entered me, as I moaned in ecstasy. Floating in the warmth of his touch was like fireworks or the heat of the candle wax running over my body. It was my emotional state becoming another. It was the connection between fun and safety, and it was security to my calmness. He was the solitude to my emptiness. He healed me once before, and I wished for that again.

I looked at things differently; everything I saw came through a new shade of colours, each more beautiful than the next. The radiance of nature was dazzling, and certain songs made me feel emotional and alive. One of my fondest memories of this new stage of healing was a hike that I was told I could no longer do. I decided I was fearless, and I would persevere. I remember looking at the stunning natural views, and the sun was shining, but it was also raining. I was wet, tired, and so very sore, but I thought to myself, if I could just keep going and make it to the top of my climb, it would be all right. Then and there, I would know I was going to be okay.

One thousand thoughts and feelings passed as I watched the sunset. All I could hear was the beating of my heavy heart. Sitting at the peak, I wondered if I could do this every day, something that I thought impossible but would try anyway; believing in myself was all that mattered. It suddenly seemed like a cosmic joke that the universe would toss life lessons my way, and ultimately, how I perceived things would determine my happiness. The way I responded to the hand dealt me was my key to peace.

Life was no longer about the failures or the anger inside me; it wasn't the sadness I carried from one place to another. Instead, life became breaking through the boundaries I needed to overcome, becoming stronger and unstoppable. Every day I chose to smile at my challenges, knowing that the very things trying to break me down were ultimately only going to make me stronger. The stroke had already transformed me, and I had overcome the greatest barrier of all: my image of myself.

I would face all the fear and darkness in the world to rediscover this place I had found. I loved the woman that I became and all that I learned in the process of my becoming. My stroke was a memory, a part of my path that was not fully revealed. As I tried to focus on the present, I felt the gifts of solitude in all aspects of my life. I no longer feared outward events of ignorance and hate because I developed some detachment from things beyond my control. In my best moments, I choose to see a learning curve in our evolution. What if what we're most afraid of is meant to save us?

When I had my awakening, the significant burden of all my fears and physical pain went away. I no longer cared what people perceived, and I was no longer attached to materialistic things. All that mattered was the love inside my soul and the peace I created for myself. My sorrow and despair became a long pathway of forgiveness. I had been trapped for years in my suffering, yet I took away the very walls of my imprisonment. Now, as I stood revelling in the sunlight, I had, at last, achieved the clarity of a child's wisdom.

Death is a stripping away of all that is not you.
The secret of life is to "die before you die "and find that there is no
death.

~Eckhart Tolle

Dear Reader

This is Your Gift of Peace

As I learned how to walk again, I tried to be very aware of the stillness surrounding me. It's always inviting me to be the silent observer of everything going on—we all really are. It was like nothing I'd ever experienced. While walking, I encountered a sense of peace and heightened wisdom by being more aware of my thoughts. I heard the birds, the wind whistling, and the rocks I kicked ahead of me. I was simultaneously aware of it all. I even noticed the space between my thoughts, and as my mind started to wander, I could bring myself back to being present.

Even though I faced so much adversity and struggled with my recovery, I was also presented with an opportunity allowing me to go forward in a different way...a better way. What looked bad at the moment had a purpose. Deep in my heart, I believe that everything happens for a reason. I don't want you to lose yourself in the fear and panic of the past. But instead to inspire you to take some time to find stillness in the present. My ask of you is to seek guidance in whatever way is right for you. If you find the courage to do what I did and take this time to look at your situation and shift your way of thinking, it will be your first step towards making your mind a better place. You will give yourself the gift of peace.

Take some time for the self-reflection on the following pages to shift your mindset around peace.

Where Can I Find Gratitude Within Peace?

What Lessons Have I Learned About Peace?

What Part of Peace Can I Release Control Of?

How Can I Accept Peace Right Now?

My Reflection Around Peace

My Poem About Peace

A Letter To Myself About Peace

Dear Self,

X

The Gift of You

My favourite part of the day
is darkness and only the
sound of my thoughts and beating heart.
Candles burn as I write and come alive
because I am not afraid of
these Shadows.
I embrace what has all come
from my mind.

~Natasha Mochrie

My mind and emotions are playing tricks on me. I've been convinced since birth that time existed as a 24-hour clock and the Gregorian calendar, and with them came the practical framework of all my daily habits and relationships. Were these tools enough? Were they the only helpful understanding of time? Our rules helped us coordinate lives worldwide despite vast differences in cultures and individuals. And yet, the mystics agree that there is no such thing as time; it is an illusion. It is a concept of mind and an agreed-upon reality, but it is also slipping through my fingers to a river that is just a dream. I am left with my memories and the sorrow of knowing time always runs out.

Nothing in my life has been worthwhile that didn't involve taking risks and stepping into the void of the unknown. Nelson

Mandela said, *there is no passion to be found playing small—in settling for a life that is less than the one you are capable of living.* My life lessons weren't taught in school and didn't end at deciding what I wanted to be when I grew up. They weren't found in the opinions of my friends and family members. The wisdom I attained came through experience and all the risks I took despite being told I wasn't capable.

My life wasn't predetermined, and how things turned out depended on my choices and how I saw the story unfolding. I chose the plot and characters. I chose passion and taking chances, thinking outside the box and not being afraid to fail. Every failed experiment brought me one step closer to success. I had to take risks! I knew failure would occur at some point in my life, and I just needed to accept it. If I stumbled and fell or felt embarrassed, I just needed to embrace that experience.

Standing at the corner of my room, I imagined myself on my deathbed waiting to follow the light home. Around me were the ghosts of my dreams and the people I once wanted in my life. When I faced going to the grave with all my what-ifs and wishes, how many ghosts would be there with time knocking at my door?

Dear Chelsie,

These letters never get easier, but in a sense, I feel at peace knowing you will read this one soon, wherever I am. I'm happy. I'm okay and watching over you. I love you. My beautiful little sister, even though you're younger than me, you're so much wiser. I am so proud of who you are today. You are one of the most beautiful souls in my life. You are a strong and amazing mom. I love that about you. I wish that I could have been a mom. I think I would have been a good one. I still have Riggs. He is my baby and my number one. I think we all sometimes forget what's most important. What if I told you tomorrow was never promised to arrive? What would you do? Chelsie, we get to choose to live fully every day until we're gone. If I had one wish, it would be for you to live a happy life where you are loved. Since my stroke, something awoke inside me, and I feel everything intensely. Life is short, and to be sad or just content in your day-to-day living isn't worth it. Thank you for always being there for me and loving me for who I am. You guide me in more ways than I could ever tell you. I will always be with you no matter where you are.

A song to remember,
a moment to share and shed a tear.

~Lana Del Ray Ft. Stevie Nicks:
Beautiful People Beautiful Problems

In writing this book, I discovered how strong I was. The knowledge was with me all along. The light and wisdom that came with this gift created new energy inside me. The laughter and the love were so deep, and the tears that flowed down my cheek came from trusting I was living with purpose.

I allowed myself to let go of time and prayers. One of the most important gifts I received was learning patience with myself and my goals. Life always led me off the path I had in mind. I was 31 years old at my lowest point, and then one day, my life changed forever: On February 2, 2020, I died, and yet, I finally started living. The risks I took, the people I met, and the people I loved gave me that second chance to live.

Save Tonight. The song that I'll remember and dance to always. I often wonder how you can feel so loved and powerful, full of serenity, and yet never satisfied because you're terrified of losing it all. Why do we never feel good enough? In the end, it wasn't the attachment I was craving, and it wasn't the sex or even how I felt. I was starving for myself to realize how powerful I was. I never needed anyone to feel those emotions; they came out because I let go. I was truly capable of anything as long as I eventually surrendered the pictures I painted in my mind. They were just illusions and futures I hadn't created yet, and always tempted me to stray from the present. But there was limitless power to the unique desires I held inside. Thank you, Ian.

I have written these ten gifts to myself, so I remember the journey it has taken me to finally arrive. Through telling my story, I hoped I could turn my traumatic experience of the stroke into something more than learning to walk again. My inner transformation came through confronting my fears of the unknown and the limbo stage of nothingness. Along the way, I discovered hope when I settled deeper into my true nature in the place where wisdom led me. This became the start of a new life of striving for acceptance and a mindful path of peace.

I am grateful I learned how to change my thoughts by understanding their power. My perspectives aligned with the energy of love, abundance, and peace, or fear, lack, and separation. I had to choose carefully where I focussed my attention. I no longer had to be a prisoner of any perspectives that didn't serve my highest good, and I didn't have to believe in anything that felt wrong. My power lay in my ability to take personal responsibility for the energy I sent out to the world.

When I aligned my energy with love, abundance, and peace, I attracted more of those qualities in my life. I needed to change my focus when I became aware of undesirable life consequences. However, I couldn't force the universe or my mind into submission. I had the power to change when I was willing to look at myself and determine if I lived by my values and alignment.

It takes effort to stay in the energy of kindness and gratitude. But it's worth the practice and reminds me it's always a choice to stay beautifully empowered. My memories with these blessings bring greater joy and peace into my life. There is a price with the gift of time. Sometimes its illusions had me thinking there would always be a tomorrow and nothing could take away certain moments, but I learned we have so little time to live genuinely. I am still growing and becoming something more every day, discovering what is precious, learning more about who I really am. While I still have a beating heart, I want to savour every day as a gift of time, love fiercely, and risk ever deeper into my soul's mysteries.

What a caterpillar calls the end of the world, we call a butterfly.

~Eckhart Tolle

Dear Reader

This is Your Gift of You

This journey we have gone through together, dear reader, has been so profound, including all these intangible chapters I have written. I hope they bring some clarity and peace to you.

It is a terrible feeling to be expected to do or complete something that you are not sure you can do. But you can! When you are yourself, you are honest about your limitations, which gives you the margin you need to maneuver and—if necessary—outsource traumas or negative emotions that you are not comfortable dealing with.

By knowing and being yourself, you can better acknowledge things that you do not know well enough. You won't be too proud to ask questions because you, and hopefully, everyone around you will work with you and not against you. Know how genuinely beautiful you are.

What Gifts About Yourself Have You Taken From
Beautifully Empowered?

In What Ways Are You Inspired By Your
Reflections, Poetry, and Thoughts?

What Small Changes Are You Ready To Make In Your Life?

If You Didn't Have Tomorrow, What Would You Do Today?

About the Author

Natasha Mochrie lives in Kelowna, BC, where she is an author, armchair philosopher, and consultant in fitness and wellness. At 31, she experienced a stroke that left her paralyzed and partially blind. Her most intimate thoughts and emotions formed the letters and journal entries that would ultimately inspire her recovery and the creation of this book. With messages on self-love and healing, Natasha's insights are seen on multiple social media platforms like Instagram, Facebook, and LinkedIn. When not working, Natasha makes memories with her dog, Big Rigg, and enjoys living room tea with cards and crystals. She also makes time for nature walks and connecting for genuine conversations.

Can fear be a gift? That isn't a question I ponder very often. I suppose one could argue various scenarios in which this feeling, one all humans have varying degrees of experience with, could be seen as a benefit when studying the big picture of our lives. What about depression? Resentment? How about just getting to the prime age of the human experience and suddenly having a stroke? It seems to get harder and harder to justify any of these things as 'gifts' the further down the rabbit hole we go. But then we encounter Natasha, and her true story forged straight from the heart. She has taken an uncommon, nearly unthinkable situation, and broken it down, detail by detail, feeling by feeling, lesson by lesson, then presented it unabashedly for the world to see. I would like to give everyone the benefit of the doubt and think that no one would wish a stroke on anybody. But they still happen, and to people in all walks of life.

Sometimes they happen to the person one would least expect, and I believe Natasha's situation would be categorized that way. A young, beautiful, spirited woman, dealing with the same issues people her age deal with: jobs, relationships, discovering who she really is, suddenly put into a dramatic, unknown trajectory. What does one do? What thoughts and feelings come with such an epic event? Is it possible to pick up the pieces that break off during such trials, and will they reattach and fit back together?

Natasha has taken her story and gone the extra mile by doing the work to answer such questions. When faced with adversity, she bravely, authentically dealt with these, and more questions that came before her, allowing her to do a deep dive on her beliefs, priorities, core values and analyze how she used to look at the world versus how she would move forward. She decided to embrace all she went through and accept everything that came as gifts. The beautiful thing about her presentation is that we can all relate to much of it...fear, resentment, depression, unexpected setbacks, and more. We can use Natasha's story as a blueprint; how to make these feelings into tools for the building project called life, a project that is never completed. A project that sometimes suffers massive setbacks, and even sometimes forces us to rebuild right from scratch. Natasha has done just that and shared the design with all of us. She did a bunch of very difficult heavy lifting, and this volume is a heartfelt, beautiful account of her experience and the gifts she received in doing so.

Mike Chisholm
Co Author of 'She Changed Me: One Ordeal, Two Perspectives' and
Host of 'He Cast' the official podcast of HeChangedIt.com

Printed in the USA
CPSIA information can be obtained
at www.ICGtesting.com
LVHW021743010224
770664LV00004B/499